Wake Up, Brain!!™

250 Brain-Stretching Challenges
for Language Arts, Math, Geography and More...

Michelle Ball & Barbara Morris

These popular teacher resources and activity books are available from
ECS Learning Systems, Inc., for Grades K-6.

Editor: Shirley J. Durst
Cover Design and Page Layout: Anh N. Le

ISBN 1-57022-229-0

Table of Contents

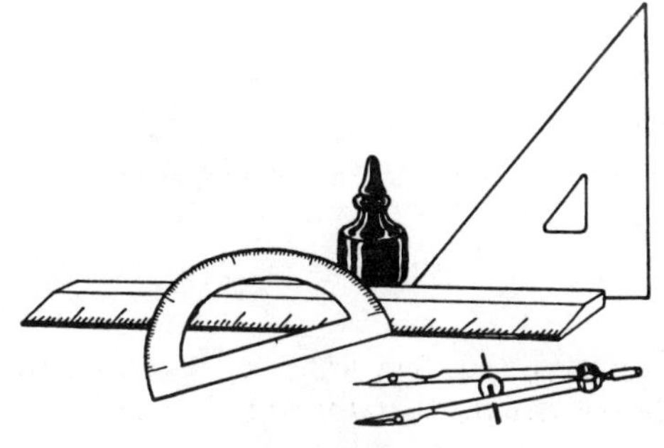

ECS Learning Systems, Inc.

Wake Up, Brain!! • Grade 6

About this Book

My inspiration for *Wake Up, Brain!!* came when I was challenged to keep track of the grammar, spelling, language, geography, and math concepts taught in my multi-age classroom. As an organizational tool, I created mini lesson plans for tracking curriculum elements for each grade or skill level. The plan included activities in five different curricular areas, plus one riddle.

My co-author, Barbara Morris, created a student- and teacher-friendly format on her computer. As time passed, we wrote more and more activities for grades 1, 2, and 3, and eventually created *Wake Up, Brain!!* for grades 4, 5, and 6, as well.

I use *Wake Up, Brain!!* as my daily mini lesson plan and expand the ideas in detail on the chalkboard or in class discussion. What a time-saver! No researching ideas or deciding what lessons to use. Students can finish all 5 activities and try to solve the riddle in as little as 5 to ten minutes.

Kids love *Wake Up, Brain!!*, too. I am constantly amazed and delighted at how practice with these mini-lessons enhances student learning in the individual subject areas. It only took a week or two for my students to get accustomed to reviewing the five subject areas at once. Now it's one of their favorite ways to learn!

Michelle Ball

                    ECS Learning Systems, Inc.

Each book in the Wake Up, Brain!! series covers the necessary elements for teaching grammar, language, spelling, geography, and math for a specific grade level. Whether you are a teacher in a traditional or multi-age classroom, a homeschooler, or a parent wanting to become more involved in your child's schoolwork, *Wake Up, Brain!!* is for you.

Use *Wake Up, Brain!!* for—

+ graded daily mini-lessons
+ teacher-led or independent practice
+ group practice
+ assessment of student skills, including special needs
+ reinforcement of essential concepts
+ homework, extra credit, or quizzes
+ acquainting parents with the basic curriculum

     ECS Learning Systems, Inc.   *Wake Up, Brain!!* • Grade 6

Wake Up, Brain!!

Name: ____

Grammar

1. we appreciated mr. carr fixing the sole of my shoe but it still squeaks

   ____

   ____

2. luckily john was not in much pane after he fell he broked his arm though

   ____

   ____

Spelling

Write the words that are spelled correctly.

3. wach   watch   wache   _______________________

4. within   witthen   wethen   _______________________

5. themsels   themselfs   themselves   _______________________

6. begen   begin   beggin   _______________________

Language

7. Write four pairs of synonyms.

   ECS Learning Systems, Inc.

Wake Up, Brain!!

Name: ____

Geography

1. What two states are outside the contiguous U.S. and what are their capital cities?

   _______________________________   _______________________________

2. Name one continent the Arctic Circle passes through.

   ____

Math

3. Write these numbers in decimal form.

   $\dfrac{90}{100}$ _______________________ $349\dfrac{4}{100}$ _______________________

   $19\dfrac{17}{100}$ _______________________ $5\dfrac{89}{100}$ _______________________

4. $82\overline{)1230}$ $77\overline{)231}$ $.24\overline{)149.328}$

DID YOU KNOW?

Skunks eat bees.

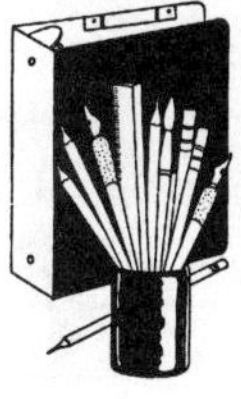

　　　ECS Learning Systems, Inc.　　　*Wake Up, Brain!!* • Grade 6　　　7

Wake Up, Brain!!

Name: _______________________________________

Grammar

1. alligators eyes stick up above its skull so their able to see above water when their bodys are under water

   ____

   ____

2. alligators is reptiles with loud voices which bellows and can be hear for grate distances

   ____

   ____

Spelling

Write the words that are spelled correctly.

3. sociaty   society   societty   _______________________

4. eagar   eager   eagger   _______________________

5. forrt   fourt   fort   _______________________

Language

Underline the verb and circle each noun.

6. This week the class studies space.

7. Doug mowed the grass.

8. Chelsea won the game of HORSE.

Wake Up, Brain!!

Name: _______________________________

Geography

1. ☐ True   ☐ False   A sea is usually larger than an ocean.

2. ☐ True   ☐ False   Land completely surrounded by water is an island.

3. ☐ True   ☐ False   If you are facing west, north is to your left.

Math

Round these numbers to the underlined place.

4. 4,<u>6</u>32   _______________________________

5. 28.0<u>3</u>5   _______________________________

6. 0.<u>2</u>73   _______________________________

DID YOU KNOW?

The venom in a daddy longlegs spider is more poisonous than a black widow spider or brown recluse.

    ECS Learning Systems, Inc.   *Wake Up, Brain!!* • Grade 6   9

Wake Up, Brain!!

Name: _______________________________

Grammar

1. alligators can not be trained so i hope that i never come a crossed 1

   ____

   ____

2. patrick was not never late for his golfing games because they loved to play

   ____

   ____

Spelling

Write the words that are spelled correctly.

3. lipps   lips   leps   _______________________

4. motor   mottor   moter   _______________________

5. shutt   shute   shut   _______________________

Language

Underline the nouns.

6. The rain made it a bad day. _______________________

7. The rain came down all night. _______________________

8. We froze in the rain and had to wear coats. _______________________

Wake Up, Brain!!

Name: _______________________________

Geography

1. If you went to the capital city, Bismarck, in what state would you be?

   ☐ Nebraska   ☐ North Dakota   ☐ South Dakota

2. If you then traveled from Bismarck to the capital of Minnesota, what direction would you travel and in what city would you be?

   ☐ north   ☐ south   ☐ east   ☐ west

   ☐ St. Paul   ☐ Minneapolis   ☐ Madison

Math

3. You have $75.25 in your pocket before you go into the store. What do you have left after you buy these items?

   ____

Compact disc	$ 15.00
T-shirt	$ 14.50
Pants	$ 32.25

4. Do you have enough left to buy three $4 burgers? _______________________

DID YOU KNOW?

Daddy longlegs spiders cannot bite humans because their jaws won't open wide enough.

        ECS Learning Systems, Inc.   *Wake Up, Brain!!* • Grade 6

Wake Up, Brain!!

Name: ____

Grammar

1. one day patrick couldnt find his golf clubs which werent not in they're bag

   ____

   ____

2. patrick didnt have no idea where they were at so he calls his coach and says he'll be late

   ____

   ____

Spelling

Write the words that are spelled correctly.

3. asleep   assleep   asleap   _______________________

4. blende   blennd   blend   _______________________

5. majic   magac   magic   _______________________

Language

6. Write the abbreviations for the last six months of the year.

   ECS Learning Systems, Inc.

Wake Up, Brain!!

Name: _______________________________

Geography

1. Where is a home game played by the Miami Dolphins?

   ❑ Colorado   ❑ Florida   ❑ Oregon

2. In what state will you find San Francisco?

   ❑ Colorado   ❑ California   ❑ Connecticut

Math

At the pet store, betas are \$3.25 each, guppies are \$1.75 each, and goldfish are \$2.10 each.

3. What is the average price of these three fish?_______________________________

4. How much would six guppies and three goldfish cost? _______________________________

5. What is the difference between the cost of ten betas and 14 guppies?_______________________

DID YOU KNOW?

On average, people fear spiders more than they fear death.

          ECS Learning Systems, Inc.   *Wake Up, Brain!!* • Grade 6   13

Wake Up, Brain!!

Name: ____

Grammar

1. patrick didnt no that he left them in his dads car or if he put them away

   ____

   ____

2. this aint a good day, cried patrick i cant never play again if i dont find my clubs

   ____

   ____

Spelling

Write the words that are spelled correctly.

3. nattiv   native   nateve   ________________________

4. knodded   nodded   noded   ________________________

5. tentt   tent   tennt   ________________________

Language

6. Write the singular form of each word below.

wolves		mice	
waxes		teeth	
echoes		parties	

     ECS Learning Systems, Inc.

Wake Up, Brain!!

Name: _______________________________

Geography

1. In what state will you find the city of Santa Fe?

   ❏ New Jersey   ❏ New Mexico   ❏ New York

2. You're going on vacation in Baton Rouge. To what state are you going?

   ❏ Louisiana   ❏ Georgia   ❏ Utah

Math

Calculate the answers.

3. 706 inches x 59 = _______________________________

4. 0.434 x 36 = _______________________________

5. 37mm x 51 = _______________________________

6. 0.159 x 3.2 = _______________________________

DID YOU KNOW?

One of the strongest muscles in the human body is the tongue.

          ECS Learning Systems, Inc.

Wake Up, Brain!!

Name: _______________________________

Grammar

1. seven twenty-seven northgate mile washington seattle 83505

   ____

   ____

2. 23 June 2003

   ____

   ____

Spelling

Write the words that are spelled correctly.

3. boiling   boilling   boilng   _______________________

4. fraktional   fractional   fractonal   _______________________

5. habbits   habits   habets   _______________________

Language

Underline the simple predicate.

6. An unknown man sent a letter to the president.

7. The small car goes very fast for its size.

8. The dog performed many tricks with ease.

   ECS Learning Systems, Inc.

Wake Up, Brain!!

Name: ____

Geography

1. Which major river flows into the Mississippi River just north of St. Louis?

   ❏ Minnesota River   ❏ Illinois River

2. What is the capital of Florida?

   ❏ Tallahassee   ❏ Orlando   ❏ Miami

Math

Write these numbers in standard form.

3. Two and forty-two thousandths _______________________________

4. Seventy-three thousandths _______________________________

DID YOU KNOW?

If you toss a penny 10,000 times, it will probably not land on heads 5,000 times. The head picture weighs more, so it ends up on the bottom more often.

        ECS Learning Systems, Inc.

Wake Up, Brain!!

Name: _______________________________________

Grammar

1. deer kasey how was you're summer vacation mine was cool because the whether was nice me and my friends went to the towns' beach right back soon

____

____

____

Spelling

Write the words that are spelled correctly.

2. porrt   port   poert   _______________

3. reflected   reflicted   reflectted   _______________

4. exxtra   extra   exttra   _______________

Language

Underline the simple subject in each sentence.

5. It moves all by itself and is blue.

6. We could win the game next Thursday.

7. Jay washed all the family cars.

Wake Up, Brain!!

Name: ____

Geography

1. What country is Mexico's closest northern neighbor?

   ❏ France   ❏ U.S.   ❏ Canada

2. Which two oceans border Europe?

   ❏ Arctic, Indian   ❏ Atlantic, Indian   ❏ Atlantic, Arctic

Math

Circle the factors of:

3. **9**   1   2   3   4   5   6   7   8   9

4. **12**   1   2   3   4   5   6   9   10   12

5. **7**   1   2   3   4   5   6   7   8   9

DID YOU KNOW?

Mel Blanc, the voice of Bugs Bunny, was allergic to carrots!

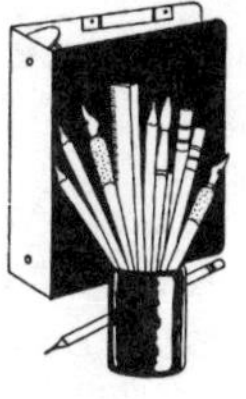

     ECS Learning Systems, Inc.   *Wake Up, Brain!!* • Grade 6   19

Wake Up, Brain!!

Name: ____

Grammar

1. at the beach i went surfing in the ocean which was to cold sometimes

   ____

   ____

2. my friends and me learnt to surf from a book called learning to surf

   ____

   ____

Spelling

Write the words that are spelled correctly.

3. harber   harba   harbor   _______________________

4. tanck   tank   tannk   _______________________

5. cofee   coffe   coffee   _______________________

Language

Complete the simile.

6. The frightened pig squealed like a _______________________________________.

7. The stars were as bright as _______________________________________.

8. His smile was as big as_______________________________________.

      ECS Learning Systems, Inc.

Wake Up, Brain!!

Name: ____

Geography

1. What is the capital city of Arizona?

   ____

2. If your friend moves to the east coast capital city of Albany, to what state has he or she moved?

   ____

Math

What is the value of 3 in each number?

3. <u>3</u>45,120 ____

4. 7,8<u>3</u>2,400 ____

5. 1<u>3</u>,692,692 ____

DID YOU KNOW?

There is no Betty Rubble in the Flintstones vitamins.

      ECS Learning Systems, Inc.   *Wake Up, Brain!!* • Grade 6

Wake Up, Brain!!

Name: _______________________________

Grammar

1. learning to surf was a great book it teached my friends and I a lot about the sport

   ____

   ____

2. maybe 1 day wel'l go to hawaii, honolulu and surf to

   ____

   ____

Spelling

Write the words that are spelled correctly.

3. sociall   social   socail   _______________________

4. swift   sweft   swifft   _______________________

5. adventre   adventure   advinture   _______________________

Language

Combine the subjects and predicates and rewrite as one sentence.

6. Jeff mowed the very long grass. Susan mowed the very long grass.

   ____

   ____

   ECS Learning Systems, Inc.

Wake Up, Brain!!

Name: _______________________________

Geography

Identify these states by their unusual shapes.

1. _______________________

2. _______________________

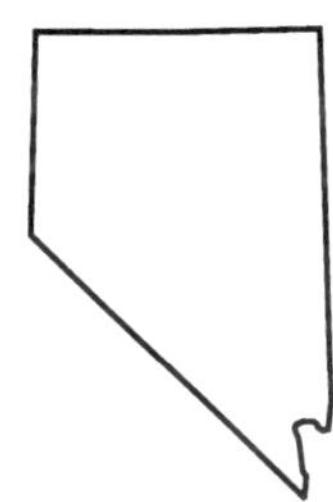

Math

Write the common factors of:

3. 10 and 12 _______________________

4. 20 and 50 _______________________

DID YOU KNOW?

Sand dunes can be more than 1,000 feet tall.

          ECS Learning Systems, Inc.   *Wake Up, Brain!!* • Grade 6   23

Wake Up, Brain!!

Name: ____

Grammar

1. dont forget to right back soon

   ____

   ____

2. ill bee waiting for the male carrier to deliver the letter in the male box of my family

   ____

   ____

Spelling

Write the words that are spelled correctly.

3. personel   perssonal   personal   _______________________

4. prise   prize   priz   _______________________

5. sunlight   sunlite   sunnlight   _______________________

Language

Rewrite the two sentences below as one sentence.

6. Julie raked all the leaves. Connie put them in a bag.

   ____

   ____

Wake Up, Brain!!

Name: _______________________________

Geography

1. What are the four directions on a compass?

   ___________________________   ___________________________

   ___________________________   ___________________________

2. ☐ True   ☐ False   Large bodies of land on Earth are called continents.

Math

Write the common factors of:

3. 8 and 12 ____

4. 7 and 13 ____

5. 5 and 25 ____

DID YOU KNOW?

In Minnesota it is illegal to cross state lines with a duck on your head!

　　　ECS Learning Systems, Inc.　　　*Wake Up, Brain!!* • Grade 6　　25

Wake Up, Brain!!

Name: ____

Grammar

1. my dad runned in these shoes this summer a lot so hes going to half to get hisself a knew pair

   ____

   ____

2. my moms running shoes are broke down she could not never wear them again

   ____

   ____

Spelling

Write the words that are spelled correctly.

3. bare   bere   baer   _______________________

4. lok   loke   lock   _______________________

5. reletions   relations   relatons   _______________________

Language

Write a compound sentence for each pair of sentences.

6. We went to the baseball game. We watched them lose.

   ____

7. We went to the fair. We rode all the rides.

   ____

Wake Up, Brain!!

Name: _______________________________

Geography

1. Name the island located off the southeast coast of Africa.

   ____

2. Name a famous river in Brazil. The river empties into the Atlantic Ocean.

   ____

Math

Solve the equations.

3. $8 \times e = 32$ e = _______________________________

4. $5m = 50$ m = _______________________________

5. $3 = 99 \div q$ q = _______________________________

DID YOU KNOW?

In Indiana it is illegal to ride public transportation for at least an hour after eating garlic.

  ECS Learning Systems, Inc.

Wake Up, Brain!!

Name: ____

Grammar

1. im sure my parent's would like me to by them for christmas each a new pare of running shoes

   ____

   ____

2. my parents run faster than i ever could. Because they run 5 times a week

   ____

   ____

Spelling

Write the words that are spelled correctly.

3. boukay   bouquat   bouquet   _______________________

4. chaen   chain   chian   _______________________

5. fetures   featores   features   _______________________

Language

Write a compound sentence for these two sentences.

6. We could go to the show. We could go bowling.

   ____

   ____

    ECS Learning Systems, Inc.

Wake Up, Brain!!

Name: _______________________________________

Geography

1. Which direction would you fly going from San Francisco, California, to Albany, New York?

   ____

2. What river would you cross to go from the United States to Mexico?

   ____

Math

3. $58 = 13 + w$ $w =$ _______________________

4. $p - 12 = 36$ $p =$ _______________________

5. $36 = 9 \times b$ $b =$ _______________________

DID YOU KNOW?

The Hundred Years' War between France and England lasted longer than 100 years.

     ECS Learning Systems, Inc.   *Wake Up, Brain!!* • Grade 6

Wake Up, Brain!!

Name: ____

Grammar

1. in france eating is a important activity each meal takes about 2 two three hours

   ____

   ____

2. the french dont just eat they dine that means they talk and enjoy other peoples company during their meals

   ____

   ____

Spelling

Write the words that are spelled correctly.

3. casle   casstle   castle   _______________________

4. hadno't   hadn't   hadnn't   _______________________

5. knocked   knoked   nocked   _______________________

Language

6. Circle C to show the noun is common or P to show it is proper.

class	C	P		Europe	C	P
France	C	P		country	C	P
teacher	C	P		school	C	P

     ECS Learning Systems, Inc.

Wake Up, Brain!!

Name: ____

Geography

1. Name the seven Central American countries.

1.	5.
2.	6.
3.	7.
4.	

Math

2. 107
    x 1.6
    ____

3. 52
    x 88
    ____

4. 0.87
    x 9
    ____

Solve for p. Circle the letter of your answer.

5. 8p = 112
   a. 898
   b. 0.14
   c. 14

6. 9p = 90
   a. 0.10
   b. 10
   c. 810

DID YOU KNOW?

A crocodile cannot stick its tongue out.

          ECS Learning Systems, Inc.

Wake Up, Brain!!

Name: ____

Grammar

1. being a waiter or waitress is a very important job in france and they deserved respect a lot

   ____

   ____

2. children in france is required to learn a different language like english or german

   ____

   ____

Spelling

Write the words that are spelled correctly.

3. meerly   merely   mearly   ___________________

4. physical   phisical   phycical   ___________________

5. strok   strooke   stroke   ___________________

Language

6. Circle C to show the noun is common or P to show it is proper.

girl	C P	Brazil	C P
Rosa	C P	Snake River	C P
continent	C P	principal	C P

Wake Up, Brain!!

Name: ____

Geography

1. The prime meridian passes through the:

   ☐ North and South Pole   ☐ United States

2. Name the large gulf on the northern coast of Australia.

   ____

Math

3. 31)¯13,715   4. 5)¯5,402

5. 22)¯6,598   6. 10)¯9,847

DID YOU KNOW?

Polar bears are left-handed.

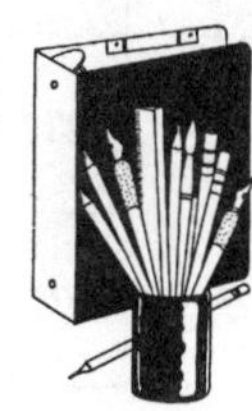

          ECS Learning Systems, Inc.   *Wake Up, Brain!!* • Grade 6   33

Wake Up, Brain!!

Name: ____

Grammar

1. france children start school at about 9 oclock and end around 330 or 4 oclock

   ____

   ____

2. the winter olympics are a world wide event them athletes from many different countrys compete

   ____

   ____

Spelling

Write the words that are spelled correctly.

3. abilety   ability   abillity   ______________________

4. defice   device   devis   ______________________

5. owner   ouner   ownor   ______________________

Language

6. Write the plural form of each noun.

deer		watch	
monkey		sheep	
wolf		berry	

        ECS Learning Systems, Inc.

Wake Up, Brain!!

Name: _______________________________________

Geography

1. In what state do the Rocky Mountains cover about 33% of the land area?

   ☐ Idaho   ☐ Montana   ☐ Wyoming

2. Name the country with the largest land area in the Eastern Hemisphere.

   ____

Math

What is the greatest common factor of these pairs of numbers?

3. 28 and 42 _____________________

4. 18 and 26 _____________________

DID YOU KNOW?

A cockroach can live nine days without its head before it starves to death.

Wake Up, Brain!!

Name: ____

Grammar

1. there is many different winter sports in the olympics skiing skating and hockey

   ____

   ____

2. in the summer olympics athletes compete in gymnastics basketball track and field and many many more sports

   ____

   ____

Spelling

Write the words that are spelled correctly.

3. tawt   taugt   taught   _______________________

4. deliteful   delightful   delightfull   _______________________

5. refrigerator   refridgerator   refrigerater   _______________________

Language

6. Write the plural form of each noun.

woman		calf	
baby		ox	
foot		tomato	

Wake Up, Brain!!

Name: ____

Geography

1. What major river runs close to the equator?

   ____

2. What is the capital of Italy?

   ____

Math

3. $9\overline{)2,304}$

4. $92\overline{)3,128}$

5. $16\overline{)32,016}$

6. $8\overline{)6,416}$

DID YOU KNOW?

The average chocolate bar has nine insect legs in it.

     ECS Learning Systems, Inc.   *Wake Up, Brain!!* • Grade 6   37

Wake Up, Brain!!

Name: ____

Grammar

1. in most olympic sports males and females they dont never compete against each others

   ____

   ____

2. olympic competition takes the hard work and the determination for the athlete's who compete in them

   ____

   ____

Spelling

Write the words that are spelled correctly.

3. weeke   weake   weak   ______________________________

4. fedaral   fedral   federal   ______________________________

5. ordinery   ordinary   ordenary   ______________________________

Language

6. Write the possessive form of the first noun in each pair.

men coats		girls hat	
fox ear		women flowers	
baby clothes		deer feet	

          ECS Learning Systems, Inc.

Wake Up, Brain!!

Name: _______________________________

Geography

1. In which direction does a latitude line run?

   ____

2. On what continent are the Himalayan Mountains?

   ____

Math

What are the prime factors for each number?

3. 57 ___________________________

4. 21 ___________________________

DID YOU KNOW?

A polar bear's skin is black. Its fur is not white, but actually, is clear.

     ECS Learning Systems, Inc.

Wake Up, Brain!!

Name: ____

Grammar

1. my teacher mrs harrison she is a great writer in fact she has published many of her storyies in magazines

   ____

   ____

2. mrs harrisons sister miss hart has wrote a book and shes only twenty two years old

   ____

   ____

Spelling

Write the words that are spelled correctly.

3. sorrey   sorey   sorry   _______________________

4. caje   cage   cagje   _______________________

5. munkey   monkey   moncky   _______________________

Language

6. Write the possessive form of the first noun in each pair.

bees honey		family car	
woman house		roses thorns	
flower petals		dog fleas	

          ECS Learning Systems, Inc.

Wake Up, Brain!!

Name: ____

Geography

1. In which direction does a longitude line run?

   ____

2. On what continent are the Andes Mountains?

   ____

Math

3. What year had the best attendance?

   ____

4. In _____________, the attendance was at an all-time low of _______________.

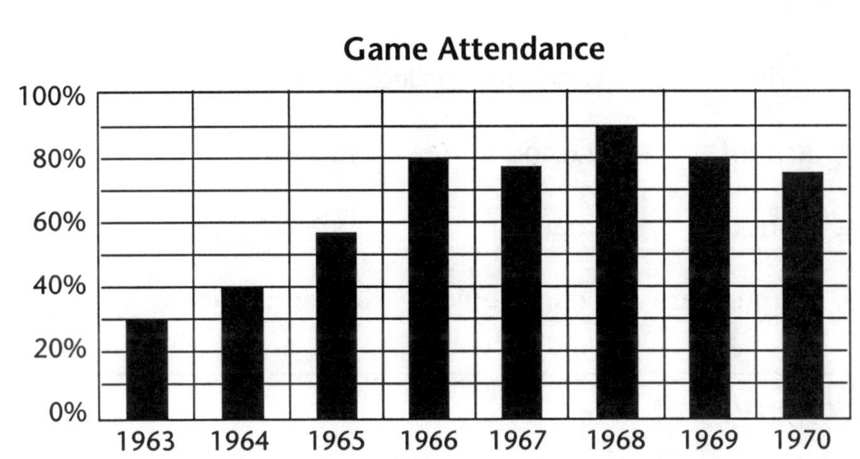

DID YOU KNOW?

A rhinoceros horn is made of compacted hair.

   ECS Learning Systems, Inc.   *Wake Up, Brain!!* • Grade 6   41

Wake Up, Brain!!

Name: ____

Grammar

1. mrs harrison teaches us on how to improve our writting skills and i try vary hard to do good

   ____

   ____

2. sometimes its hard putting them adjectives in front of them nouns but it helps my writing buy 100%

   ____

   ____

Spelling

Write the words that are spelled correctly.

3. acount   account   acounnt   _______________________

4. borred   baord   board   _______________________

5. comunicate   communicate   communnicate   _______________________

Language

A **direct object** is a noun that receives the action of the verb. Underline the direct object in each sentence.

6. The captain saw a lighthouse on the cliff.

7. A sailor spotted a dolphin.

8. The captain steered the ship.

    ECS Learning Systems, Inc.

 # Wake Up, Brain!! 

Name: ___________________________________

Geography

1. On what continent is the Nile River?

   ____

2. What is the capital of Texas?

   ____

Math

3.   9.01
     × 5
     ______

4.   2.03
     × 22
     ______

5.   3.012
     × 11
     ______

DID YOU KNOW?

Donald Duck comics were banned in Finland because Donald doesn't wear pants.

   ECS Learning Systems, Inc.   *Wake Up, Brain!!* • Grade 6   43

Wake Up, Brain!!

Name: ____

Grammar

1. this summer i will travel a cross the pacific ocean with my freind mr jacobs to places like maui

   ____

   ____

2. mark s jacob's is a vary accomplished ship captain who's name is known through out the us

   ____

   ____

Spelling

Write the words that are spelled correctly.

3. mirrer   mirror   mirrar   _______________________

4. outline   otline   outlinne   _______________________

5. dekc   decke   deck   _______________________

Language

Underline the direct object in the following sentences.

6. Each second grade class visits three stores.

7. One student makes necklaces.

8. The other student builds birdhouses.

   ECS Learning Systems, Inc.

Wake Up, Brain!!

Name: _______________________________

Geography

1. On which continent is the Chang Jiang River?

   ____

2. Does the prime meridian pass through Spain?

   ❏ Yes   ❏ No

Math

Indicate the correct sign for **less than** or **greater than**.

3. $\dfrac{4}{7}$ __________ 1

4. $\dfrac{18}{12}$ __________ 1

5. $\dfrac{15}{10}$ __________ 1

6. $\dfrac{37}{96}$ __________ 1

DID YOU KNOW?

"Stewardesses" is the longest word which can be typed with only the left hand.

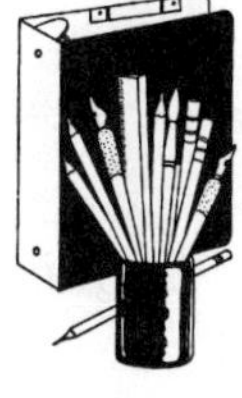

          ECS Learning Systems, Inc.   *Wake Up, Brain!!* • Grade 6

Wake Up, Brain!!

Name: ____

Grammar

1. him and i are going to start in california, san francisco and end up in hawaii

   ____

   ____

2. it is going too be a vary long trip, may be to long for me

   ____

   ____

Spelling

Write the words that are spelled correctly.

3. polise   police   poliec   _______________________

4. species   spesies   spieces   _______________________

5. stranger   strangar   stragger   _______________________

Language

Underline the sentences that have a direct object.

6. The campers set up the tent.

7. The lamp flashed brightly.

8. Julie called loudly.

     ECS Learning Systems, Inc.

Wake Up, Brain!!

Name: ___________________________

Geography

1. In what continent is the Huang He River?

   ____

2. Does the prime meridian pass through Portugal?

   ☐ Yes   ☐ No

Math

Find each quotient.

3. $5\overline{)4}$

4. $500\overline{)400}$

5. $30\overline{)27}$

6. $4.20\overline{)21.00}$

DID YOU KNOW?

If you keep a goldfish in a dark room, it will eventually turn white.

          ECS Learning Systems, Inc.   *Wake Up, Brain!!* • Grade 6   47

Wake Up, Brain!!

Name: _______________________________

Grammar

1. it will be vary exciting to sea all the places on the way and i get to meet mr jacobs' cousin

   ____

   ____

2. mr jacobs' cousin misses montgomery lives in hawaii and can speak for languages

   ____

   ____

Spelling

Write the words that are spelled correctly.

3. elektrons   electoens   electrons   _______________

4. foriegn   foreign   foregin   _______________

5. fout   foght   fought   _______________

Language

Draw a line under the adverbs.

6. The birds are singing cheerfully.

7. We have awakened bright and early.

8. The horses will run gracefully.

   Wake Up, Brain!! • Grade 6   ECS Learning Systems, Inc.

Wake Up, Brain!!

Name: _______________________________

Geography

1. Where is the Hudson Bay?

   ____

2. At what strait does the Mediterranean Sea meet the Atlantic Ocean?

   ____

Math

Round each number to the given place.

3. 54.69   (tenths)   _______________________

4. 7.683   (hundredths) _______________________

5. 139.887   (ones)   _______________________

DID YOU KNOW?

Women blink nearly twice as often as men.

          ECS Learning Systems, Inc.   *Wake Up, Brain!!* • Grade 6

 # Wake Up, Brain!! 

Name: _______________________________

Grammar

1. he asked wear are you going on sun oct eighth

    ____

    ____

2. im not going anywhere on Sunday but on Monday im going to the fare

    ____

    ____

Spelling

Write the words that are spelled correctly.

3. industrial   indostrial   industreal   _____________________

4. accedent   accident   aciddent   _____________________

5. depertment   departmant   department   _____________________

Language

Write the past tense form of each verb.

6. blow ____

7. freeze ____

8. write ____

9. sing ____

10. speak ____

   Wake Up, Brain!! • Grade 6   ECS Learning Systems, Inc.

Wake Up, Brain!!

Name: _______________________________

Geography

1. What countries border the Gulf of Mexico?

   ____

2. The Bering Strait separates what two continents?

   _______________________   _______________________

Math

Solve each problem. Show your work.

3. $0.604 \div 0.2 =$ _______________

4. $35.852 \div 4 =$ _______________

DID YOU KNOW?

The sentence, "The quick brown fox jumps over the lazy dog," uses every letter in the English alphabet.

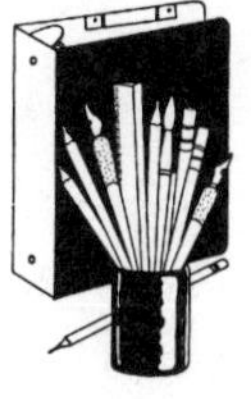

     ECS Learning Systems, Inc.

Wake Up, Brain!!

Name: ____

Grammar

1. dear mr fritz im righting too you regarding our talk last april you said you wood take the 5th grade glass to washington dc four the weekend the weekend of October 2 wood be best from mrs amanda morgan. Sincerely

____

____

____

Spelling

Write the words that are spelled correctly.

2. flash   flach   flassh   ___________________________

3. whenevor   whenever   wenever   ___________________________

4. graed   grade   grad   ___________________________

Language

Write the present tense form of each verb.

5. studied ___________________________   6. fixed ___________________________

7. fished ___________________________   8. cried ___________________________

9. watched ___________________________   10. washed ___________________________

   Wake Up, Brain!! • Grade 6   ECS Learning Systems, Inc.

Wake Up, Brain!!

Name: ____

Geography

1. Which country has more land, the U.S. or Russia?

   ____

2. What state is north of Pennsylvania?

   ____

Math

3. The soccer team won 11 out of 27 games. How many wins did they average? Show your work.

4. It is now 1:30 p.m. What time will it be in 11 hours and 22 minutes?

   ____

DID YOU KNOW?

The names of all but two of the continents end with the same letter they start with.

　　　ECS Learning Systems, Inc.　　　*Wake Up, Brain!!* • Grade 6　　53

Wake Up, Brain!!

Name: _______________________________

Grammar

1. have you ever ben starstruck it means you have a desire two bee onstage or two preform

   ____

   ____

2. as you're debut in the school talent show approaches you're eagerness is over-taken by nervous tension

   ____

   ____

Spelling

Write the words that are spelled correctly.

3. perform   preform   prefarm   _______________________

4. librarry   libarry   library   _______________________

5. wolfes   wolvs   wolves   _______________________

Language

6. Change each pronoun to agree with the verb.

They is here.	
He are fine.	
He were fine.	
Both was good.	

Wake Up, Brain!!

Name: ____

Geography

1. The line of longitude circles the globe in which directions?

   ❏ east and west   ❏ north and south

2. What famous mountain range is found in South America?

   ____

Math

3. What year had the worst attendance?

   ____

4. In 1970, attendance was what percent higher than 1964?

   _______________.

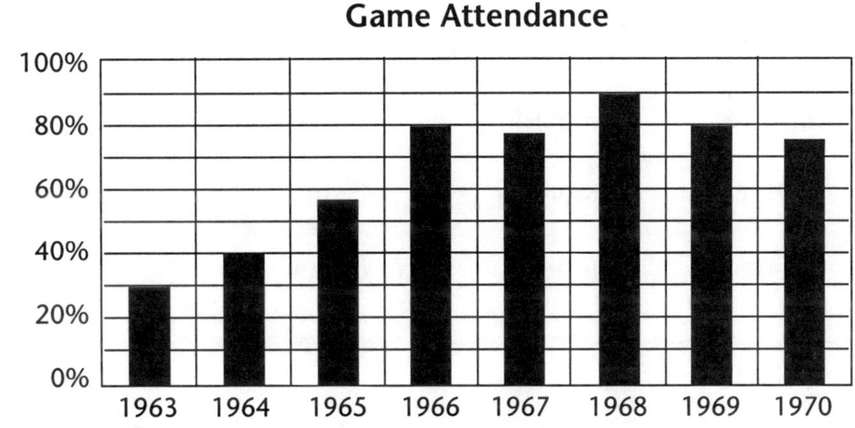

DID YOU KNOW?

The word "lethologica" describes the state of not being able to remember a word.

          ECS Learning Systems, Inc.   *Wake Up, Brain!!* • Grade 6

Wake Up, Brain!!

Name: _______________________________

Grammar

1. it will be sew exciting to sea all the countrys in europe on hour families trip this summer

   ____

   ____

2. hour cousin who can speak english french and german is going their with us

   ____

   ____

Spelling

Write the words that are spelled correctly.

3. maybee   maybe   maibee   _______________________________

4. fuchur   fewture   future   _______________________________

5. fiftene   fiteen   fifteen   _______________________________

Language

Add an adverb to each sentence.

6. The girls are singing _______________________________.

7. We slept _______________________________.

8. The geese flew by _______________________________.

Wake Up, Brain!!

Name: ____

Geography

1. The Hudson Bay is in:

   ☐ the U.S.   ☐ Canada   ☐ England

2. Where is Ellis Island?

   ☐ New Jersey   ☐ New York   ☐ Delaware

Math

Using **n** for the variable, write a multiplication expression for each situation.

3. 12 boxes of tissue, **n** boxes in a case   _______________________________

4. The number of seats on a 12-car train   _______________________________

5. Each student pays $6 for the movie   _______________________________

DID YOU KNOW?

TYPEWRITER is the longest word which can be typed using the letters on only one row of the keyboard.

        ECS Learning Systems, Inc.   *Wake Up, Brain!!* • Grade 6   57

Wake Up, Brain!!

Name: ____

Grammar

1. wear were you on december 31 1999 when the knew century began

   ____

   ____

2. memorys like them will last a life time

   ____

   ____

Spelling

Write the words that are spelled correctly.

3. thermus   thermas   thermos   _______________________

4. diktionnary   dictionary   dictionery   _______________________

5. maintinance   maintanence   maintenance   _______________________

Language

6. Correct the verb so it agrees with the subject of the sentence.

   We was going.   ____

   They is gone.   ____

   I are tired.   ____

   She seen me.   ____

   ECS Learning Systems, Inc.

Wake Up, Brain!!

Name: _______________________________

Geography

1. The Gulf of Mexico touches the U.S.

   ☐ True   ☐ False

2. What waterway separates Asia and North America?

   ____

Math

3. A pharmacist measures medicine by putting the medicine in a dish and placing the dish on a scale. The mass of the dish and the medicine is 21.4502 grams. The mass of the dish alone is 17.9836 grams. What is the mass of the medicine?

   ____

DID YOU KNOW?

If the population of China walked past you in single file, the line would never end because of the country's rate of reproduction.

  ECS Learning Systems, Inc. *Wake Up, Brain!!* • Grade 6

Wake Up, Brain!!

Name: ____

Grammar

1. stephanie and me went camping in wyoming and her and me also went in her dads camper

   ____

   ____

2. she goes were gonna have a grate time and i go i think were gonna freeze

   ____

   ____

Spelling

Write the words that are spelled correctly.

3. formula   farmula   formulae   _______________________

4. meashure   measure   mesure   _______________________

5. potato   potatoe   potatto   _______________________

Language

6. Write the present tense form of each verb.

mowed		meant	
copied		drank	
worked		sealed	
seen		went	

     ECS Learning Systems, Inc.

Wake Up, Brain!!

Name: ________________________________

Geography

1. Russia has more land than the U.S.

   ☐ True   ☐ False

2. What states are on the southern border of Pennsylvania?

   ____

Math

Write the sum or difference.

3.   134.40
      – 25.0587

4.   5.6307
      + 2.0824

5.   5.5
      198.7744
      + 63.02

6.   14.104
      0.35
      + 6.7

DID YOU KNOW?

A snail can sleep for three years.

  ECS Learning Systems, Inc. *Wake Up, Brain!!* • Grade 6 61

Wake Up, Brain!!

Name: ____

Grammar

1. whats you're favorite thing to do win its raining katherine ask as she heard the sound of thunder

   ____

   ____

2. "i like too curl up in an blanket and watch movies i answered."

   ____

   ____

Spelling

Write the words that are spelled correctly.

3. obay   obey   odey   _______________________

4. ocean   ochun   osean   _______________________

5. pome   poam   poem   _______________________

Language

6. If you are from Africa, you are _______________________

7. If you are from Poland, you are _______________________

8. If you are from England, you are _______________________

9. If you are from the USA, you are _______________________

Wake Up, Brain!!

Name: ____

Geography

Name the continent on which you will find the:

1. Himalayan Mountains ____

2. Andes Mountains ____

3. Adirondack Mountains ____

Math

4. Complete the table.

Average Water Usage Per Person in U.S.		
Gallons Per Day	Gallons Per Week	Gallons Per Year
60		

DID YOU KNOW?

The electric chair was invented by a dentist.

     ECS Learning Systems, Inc.

Wake Up, Brain!!

Name: ____

Grammar

1. ben ask what is your favorite movie do you like comedy drama or science fiction

   ____

   ____

2. my favorite is comedys cause they make you feel happy especially when its raining

   ____

   ____

Spelling

Write the words that are spelled correctly.

3. owner   ownar   ownre   _______________________

4. progrum   program   porgram   _______________________

5. owoke   awoak   awoke   _______________________

Language

Write the present tense form of each verb.

6. gone _______________________

7. taught _______________________

8. saw _______________________

Wake Up, Brain!!

Name: _______________________________

Geography

1. Name the island on the southeast coast of China.

   ____

2. What large mountain range runs through the eastern U.S.?

   ____

Math

Write the first five multiples of these numbers.

3. 5   _______________________________

4. 8   _______________________________

5. 17   _______________________________

6. 20   _______________________________

DID YOU KNOW?

You share your birthday with at least nine million other people in the world.

     ECS Learning Systems, Inc.   *Wake Up, Brain!!* • Grade 6   65

Wake Up, Brain!!

Name: ____

Grammar

1. to be or not to be that is the question these are famous lines from hamlet a play wrote by william shakespear

   ____

   ____

2. william shakespear rote many plays during his lifetime. Including romeo and juliet

   ____

   ____

Spelling

Write the words that are spelled correctly.

3. lisense lisence license _______________________________

4. promp promt prompt _______________________________

5. enginer engineer enjineer _______________________________

Language

Rewrite each phrase. Write the first noun of each phrase in possessive form.

6. children books ____________________________________

7. jar lid ____

8. deer antlers ______________________________________

  ECS Learning Systems, Inc.

Wake Up, Brain!!

Name: ____

Geography

1. What is the name of the narrow passageway between Europe and Africa?

   ____

2. Portugal is located west of which European country?

   ____

Math

3. What year saw the greatest attendance?

   ____

4. Between what years did the attendance improve the most?

   ____

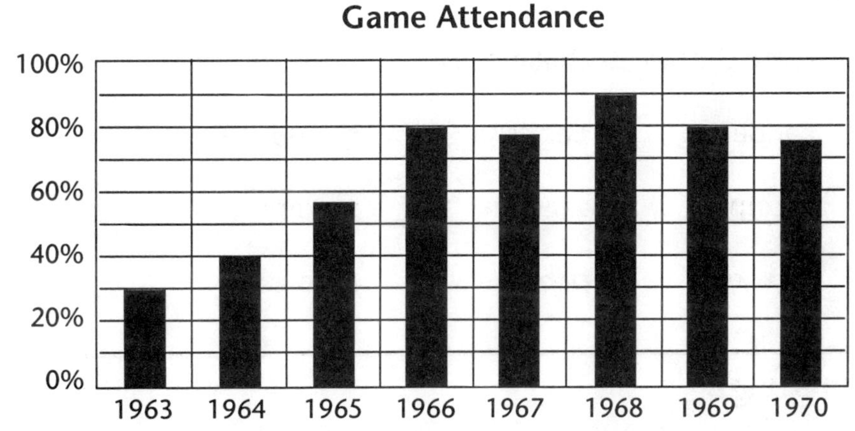

DID YOU KNOW?

"I am" is the shortest sentence with a complete subject and predicate in the English language.

     ECS Learning Systems, Inc.

Wake Up, Brain!!

Name: _______________________________

Grammar

1. romeo and juliet is about too children from opposing families the capulets and montagues who fell in love

   ____

   ____

2. in the end juliet drunk poison to make her look dead so she could run away with romeo

   ____

   ____

Spelling

Write the words that are spelled correctly.

3. bandanna   bandana   banndana   _______________________

4. vaccum   vacuum   vacumme   _______________________

5. pansy   pansey   pansie   _______________________

Language

Rewrite each phrase. Write the first noun of each phrase in possessive form.

6. team coaches   ____

7. stores signs   ____

8. spoon handle   ____

          ECS Learning Systems, Inc.

Wake Up, Brain!!

Name: _______________________________

Geography

1. What famous river flows from its source in Burundi through Cairo, Egypt?

   ____

2. What sea is near Cairo, Egypt?

   ____

Math

Solve the equations.

3. $5x = 35$ $x =$ _______________

4. $49 = 7n$ $n =$ _______________

5. $m \cdot 5 = 150$ $m =$ _______________

DID YOU KNOW?

The Eisenhower Highway interstate system requires that one mile in every five is straight. Straight sections can be used as airstrips in case of war or other emergencies.

     ECS Learning Systems, Inc.

Wake Up, Brain!!

Name: _______________________________

Grammar

1. romeo didnt get the message that juliets death was fake so he drunk poison to and died

____

____

2. when juliet awoke she found romeo dead and take a dagger and stab herself

____

____

Spelling

Write the words that are spelled correctly.

3. corse   kourse   course   _______________________

4. develope   develop   develup   _______________________

5. radical   radicle   radacle   _______________________

Language

Write the plural form of each noun.

6. woman   _______________________

7. calf   _______________________

8. baby   _______________________

9. tomato   _______________________

     ECS Learning Systems, Inc.

Wake Up, Brain!!

Name: _______________________________________

Geography

1. Name the continents that touch the Pacific Ocean.

   ____

   ____

2. Georgia is south of Florida.

   ☐ True   ☐ False

Math

3. Will Rebecca do 250 sit-ups in eight days if she does 30 each day?

   ☐ yes   ☐ no

4. Is $225 enough for 6 sweaters if each sweater costs $42?

   ☐ yes   ☐ no, $________________ more is needed.

DID YOU KNOW?

The African pygmy shrew is only 2.5 inches long from the tip of its nose to the end of its tail.

          ECS Learning Systems, Inc.   *Wake Up, Brain!!* • Grade 6

Wake Up, Brain!!

Name: _______________________________

Grammar

1. i started re-counting the amazing avents of the nite before; and a huge grin take over my face

   ____

   ____

2. it is a cool evening during the sumer win i was a mischeivous 9 year old

   ____

   ____

Spelling

Write the words that are spelled correctly.

3. geuss   gusse   guess   _______________________________

4. shelfes   shelves   shelvs   _______________________________

5. sakrifice   sacrifise   sacrifice   _______________________________

Language

What are the simple compound predicates in each sentence?

6. The snow fell from the sky and settled on the trees.

   ____

7. I stomped, yelled, and jumped for joy.

   ____

     ECS Learning Systems, Inc.

Wake Up, Brain!!

Name: ____

Geography

1. Argentina is on the North American continent.

   ❏ True   ❏ False

2. The Arctic Ocean borders most of the London coastline.

   ❏ True   ❏ False

Math

3. If Steve rides his bicycle 1000 km in June, will he bike 28 km each day?

   ❏ Yes   ❏ No, he must ride _____________ per day.

4. Starting on Monday, Stephanie does 55 jumping jacks each day. Does she do 200 by Thursday night?

   ❏ Yes   ❏ No, she will have done _______________.

DID YOU KNOW?

There are approximately ten million laws in effect to uphold the Ten Commandments.

          ECS Learning Systems, Inc.   *Wake Up, Brain!!* • Grade 6

Wake Up, Brain!!

Name: ____

Grammar

1. know one was talking and we was as board as a librarian with know books to reed

   ____

   ____

2. desperate to sizzle up our evening. We decide to take a walk in our queit; peacfull neighboor hood

   ____

   ____

Spelling

Write the words that are spelled correctly.

3. create   kreate   kreeate   _______________________

4. desparate   desperate   despirate   _______________________

5. memorys   memories   memoryes   _______________________

Language

Underline the direct object in each sentence.

6. Andrea turned in Friday's homework.

7. I read my poem's title to Dad.

8. He washed his new car very carefully.

Wake Up, Brain!!

Name: ____

Geography

1. Europe is larger than Asia.

   ❏ True   ❏ False

2. The largest ocean is the Arctic Ocean.

   ❏ True   ❏ False

Math

Write the value of the underlined digit in word form.

3. 9<u>3</u>,084,339   _______________________________

4. 16,5<u>5</u>5,200   _______________________________

5. <u>7</u>7, 325,098   _______________________________

DID YOU KNOW?

There are 266 words in the Declaration of Independence, 297 words in the Gettysburg Address, and 26,911 words in a federally-funded research paper on the price of cabbage in the United States.

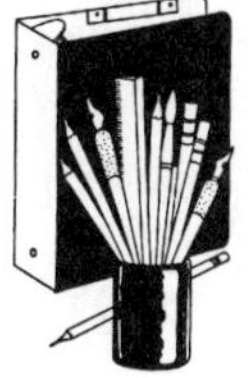

          ECS Learning Systems, Inc.   *Wake Up, Brain!!* • Grade 6   75

Wake Up, Brain!!

Name: _______________________________

Grammar

1. wile sauntering down the side walk. We noticed to muddy girls being sprade with a hose?

   ____

   ____

2. "hey what happened two you to i asked as me and ashley approached them.

   ____

   ____

Spelling

Write the words that are spelled correctly.

3. citys   cities   citeys   _______________________

4. centurys   centureys   centuries   _______________________

5. dairies   dairys   daireys   _______________________

Language

Write a homophone for each word.

6. seem   ____

7. tax   ____

8. hours   ____

Wake Up, Brain!!

Name: ____

Geography

1. The Appalachian Mountains are in the northwestern United States.

   ❑ True   ❑ False

2. The Rocky Mountains run through Idaho.

   ❑ True   ❑ False

Math

1 box pasta	$0.78
1 can tomato paste	$0.43
1 can of coffee	$2.88
1 cheese pack	$3.15

3. Can you buy three cans of tomato paste with $1? ❑ Yes ❑ No

4. Can you buy six boxes of pasta with $5?   ❑ Yes ❑ No

5. Can you buy two packs of cheese with $6.50?   ❑ Yes ❑ No

6. Can you buy five cans of coffee with $10?   ❑ Yes ❑ No

DID YOU KNOW?

It took two scientists 409 attempts to perfect the formula for the all-purpose cleaner, "409."

          ECS Learning Systems, Inc.

Wake Up, Brain!!

Name: ____

Grammar

1. we was having a mudd restling contest with a group of people inn the dirt feilds said won girl

   ____

   ____

2. i and ashley glanced at each other; we new this were the perfect chance to liven up our night

   ____

   ____

Spelling

Write the words that are spelled correctly.

3. marryed   married   maried   _______________________

4. countrys   countreys   countries   _______________________

5. surround   serround   shurround   _______________________

Language

Underline the verb and circle **T** if it is transitive or **I** if it is intransitive.

6. She drew pictures for the class.   T   I

7. The class laughed uncontrollably.   T   I

8. Soon Mrs. Ball was frustrated with the class.   T   I

9. The goldfish ate the guppy.   T   I

    ECS Learning Systems, Inc.

Wake Up, Brain!!

Name: _______________________________

Geography

1. What continent surrounds the South Pole?

   ____

2. The Arctic Circle passes through Greenland.

   ☐ True   ☐ False

Math

3. It takes Earth one year to travel around the sun. It takes Mercury 0.24 Earth years to travel around the sun. How much longer does it take Earth to travel around the sun? Show your work.

   ____

   ____

DID YOU KNOW?

Americans spell the sound of a sneeze, "Ah-choo!"; Italians spell it, "Ekchee!"; Japanese spell it, "Hakshon!"

Wake Up, Brain!!

Name: ____

Grammar

1. after ours of playing we decided too go home because it was getting dark and it was getting cold

   ____

   ____

2. as it got darker we begun running to my home because the nite was to scary

   ____

   ____

Spelling

Write the words that are spelled correctly.

3. lying   leying   lyeing   _______________________

4. mexture   mixture   mixchure   _______________________

5. stich   stitch   stitche   _______________________

Language

Use **HAS** or **HAVE** correctly in each sentence.

6. Each jogger _______________________________ trained for months.

7. A doctor _______________________________ examined the room.

8. They _______________________________ a nice, new house.

    ECS Learning Systems, Inc.

Wake Up, Brain!!

Name: ____

Geography

1. Name the seven continents of the world.

Math

Write an equation and solve for the number of days there are in:

2. three weeks _______________________________________

3. six weeks ____

4. 15 weeks ____

DID YOU KNOW?

Want to live for one trillion seconds? Not unless you want to live 31,688 years!

        ECS Learning Systems, Inc.   *Wake Up, Brain!!* • Grade 6   81

Wake Up, Brain!!

Name: ____

Grammar

1. lets go ashley screamed and we ran are fastest to the dirt feilds

   ____

   ____

2. when we got they're we saw the beutiful pool of mud and we both jumped in together at the same time

   ____

   ____

Spelling

Write the words that are spelled correctly.

3. disloyel   disloyal   desloyal   _______________________

4. prononce   pronounce   pronounse   _______________________

5. heard   haerd   hered   _______________________

Language

Underline the prefix and describe how it changes the word's meaning.

6. unhappy   ____

7. mislead   ____

8. research   ____

     ECS Learning Systems, Inc.

Wake Up, Brain!!

Name: _______________________________

Geography

1. Where is the Golden Gate Bridge?

   ____

2. Mexico has more land than the United States.

   ☐ True   ☐ False

Math

Convert ounces to pounds.

3. 32 ounces = _______________________________ pounds

4. 80 ounces = _______________________________ pounds

5. 176 ounces = _______________________________ pounds

DID YOU KNOW?

A trash collector in Massachusetts found an empty cup from a big fast food chain in a dumpster. The peel-off sticker, still intact on the cup, brought the man the $200,000 Grand Prize from a company campaign.

          ECS Learning Systems, Inc.   *Wake Up, Brain!!* • Grade 6

Wake Up, Brain!!

Name: ____

Grammar

1. the cool mud felt so good bitween are toes and we begun laughing at how much fun we was having.

   ____

   ____

2. since we was all ready too muddy pigs i decided it could'nt hurt too start a mud throwing fite

   ____

   ____

Spelling

Write the words that are spelled correctly.

3. invieted   invited   invitted   _______________________

4. pioneres   pioneers   pianeers   _______________________

5. predukit   predicit   predicate   _______________________

Language

Write the past tense form of each verb.

6. carry ____

7. study ____

8. destroy ____

Wake Up, Brain!!

Name: ____

Geography

1. Which hemisphere has more water?

   ❏ eastern   ❏ western

2. The Tropic of Cancer passes through which continents?

   ❏ North America   ❏ South America   ❏ Asia

   ❏ Africa   ❏ Europe   ❏ Antarctica

Math

Write an equation and solve for how many dimes you can get with:

3. 32 nickels _______________________________________

4. 40 nickels _______________________________________

5. 100 nickels ______________________________________

DID YOU KNOW?

Do you have any Grey Poupon? Mr. Grey invented the mustard, and Mr. Poupon invested the money to build the factory.

          ECS Learning Systems, Inc.   *Wake Up, Brain!!* • Grade 6

Wake Up, Brain!!

Name: ____

Grammar

1. finally! We got too my house and sitted down to rest on the steps. Because we was out of breath from hour run

   ____

   ____

2. we must of dozed. Because win we waked up the mud on our skin has dryed

   ____

   ____

Spelling

Write the words that are spelled correctly.

3. remind   remmind   reamind   _____________________

4. reaptiles   reptiels   reptiles   _____________________

5. capptured   captured   captered   _____________________

Language

Underline the correct helping verb.

6. I (have, has) watched two movies.

7. The workers (has, had) traveled many miles.

8. Jenny will (has, have) a little brother soon.

  ECS Learning Systems, Inc.

Wake Up, Brain!!

Name: ____

Geography

1. Name the earth's four oceans.

2. Circle the two oceans in #1's answer that border Europe.

Math

Kenny saved $138.00.

3. Does he have enough money to buy a jacket for $78, a skateboard for $22, two CDs for $17 each, and a hamburger basket for $3.75 each for himself and his friend?

    ❏ Yes, he'll have $_______________ left over.

    ❏ No, he'll be $_______________ short.

DID YOU KNOW?

One winner of the Odd Title Award for the most unusual book title:
Reusing Old Graves: A Study of Cemetery Etiquette.

     ECS Learning Systems, Inc.

Wake Up, Brain!!

Name: _______________________________

Grammar

1. we got out the hose well ashley says lets get started washing our selfs off

____

____

2. this sure hasnt been a boaring night i screamed with laughter as she spraid me with water

____

____

Spelling

Write the words that are spelled correctly.

3. comunication   communication   comunicasion   _______________________________

4. losse   loose   looce   _______________________________

5. difer   deffer   differ   _______________________________

Language

Write the past tense form of these verbs.

6. describe _______________________________

7. fall _______________________________

8. make _______________________________

Wake Up, Brain!!

Name: ____

Geography

1. The South Pole is located on the continent of:

   ☐ Asia   ☐ Antarctica   ☐ South America

2. Which two continents make up a single large mass of land?

   ☐ Asia   ☐ Africa   ☐ Europe   ☐ Australia

Math

3. Sales tax in Idaho is 5%. What is the sales tax on an item that sells for $25.00?

   ____

4. 33.20 x 7.5 = ____

DID YOU KNOW?

If you take a close look at Mona Lisa, you'll see she has no eyebrows. It was the fashion of Renaissance Italy to shave them off.

          ECS Learning Systems, Inc.   *Wake Up, Brain!!* • Grade 6

Wake Up, Brain!!

Name: ____

Grammar

1. i walked in too the room and seen that the bed had'nt not even been made, yet.

   ____

   ____

2. you hasnt just got up have you jimmy i call in two the bath room

   ____

   ____

Spelling

Write the words that are spelled correctly.

3. diveing   diving   divving   _______________________

4. grined   griened   grinned   _______________________

5. pakage   pakedge   package   _______________________

Language

Write the past tense form of each verb.

6. say   ____

7. fly   ____

8. bring ____

          ECS Learning Systems, Inc.

Wake Up, Brain!!

Name: ____

Geography

1. What is the largest ocean in the world?

   ____

2. Which state has a longer ocean border? ☐ Washington   ☐ California

3. What ocean borders both of these states? ____

Math

Divide.

4. 406 ÷ 4 = ____

5. 1,256 ÷ 6 = ____

6. 17.50 ÷ 5 = ____

DID YOU KNOW?

Harvard College was named after a Puritan minister, John Harvard, after he willed his library of 400 books to the college that was then only two years old.

     ECS Learning Systems, Inc.   *Wake Up, Brain!!* • Grade 6

Wake Up, Brain!!

Name: _______________________________

Grammar

1. my brother jimmy is vary lazy. And sum times he dont get up until the after noon

   ____

   ____

2. jimmy called to me from the bath room ill be ready inn too minutes i promise

   ____

   ____

Spelling

Write the words that are spelled correctly.

3. medecine   medicine   medisine   _______________________

4. construction   constructoin   constructon   _______________________

5. gradaully   gradually   graddully   _______________________

Language

Underline the adjectives. On the line write a new adjective that changes the meaning of the sentence.

6. Some toy parts are sharp. _______________________________________

7. The man bought a new car. _____________________________________

8. Ben has long, brown hair. ______________________________________

          ECS Learning Systems, Inc.

Wake Up, Brain!!

Name: ____

Geography

What is the capital city of:

1. Kentucky? _______________________________________

2. California? ______________________________________

3. Delaware? _______________________________________

Math

4. It is 11:55 a.m. and Josh's flight to Miami leaves at 7:38 p.m. How much time does he have to get ready and get on the flight?

   ____

5. Kids should try to get ten hours of sleep each night. If you must get up at 6:15 a.m., what time should you go to bed?

   ____

DID YOU KNOW?

Ten years before the Pilgrims arrived on the Mayflower, the population of the American colonies was 350.

   ECS Learning Systems, Inc.   *Wake Up, Brain!!* • Grade 6

Wake Up, Brain!!

Name: ____

Grammar

1. well hurry cause wer'e late enough as it is i shouted and runned from the room to get my back pack

   ____

   ____

2. i try every morning to reed the news paper to sea hows my town doing?

   ____

   ____

Spelling

Write the words that are spelled correctly.

3. specifik   specific   spacific   _______________________

4. trunk   trunck   trunke   _______________________

5. outher   athor   author   _______________________

Language

Underline the adjectives in these sentences.

6. Most major projects require several tools to do a good job.

7. The red apple was totally covered with ugly worms.

8. TV programs have many excellent actors while others seem poorly trained.

Wake Up, Brain!!

Name: _______________________________

Geography

What is the capital city of:

1. Rhode Island? _______________________________

2. Oregon? _______________________________

3. Georgia? _______________________________

Math

4. It takes 2 hours and 45 minutes to get from your house to your grandmother's cabin. What time do you have to leave if she expects you at 1:30 p.m?

   ____

5. It's Tuesday at 3:15 p.m. It's been 35 hours and 28 minutes since you've seen your girlfriend. When did you last see her?

   ____

DID YOU KNOW?

The largest cells in the human body are a type of blood cell found in bone marrow. The smallest cells are brain cells.

     ECS Learning Systems, Inc.   *Wake Up, Brain!!* • Grade 6   95

Wake Up, Brain!!

Name: ____

Grammar

1. john is ten and loves to play basket ball, every day after skool he played four ours til it was dinner time

   ____

   ____

2. won day john will became a good basket ball player. Because he practice's so much

   ____

   ____

Spelling

Write the words that are spelled correctly.

3. outer   oter   outter   _______________________

4. pummp   puomp   pump   _______________________

5. soung   song   songe   _______________________

Language

Underline the descriptive adjectives in these sentences.

6. The hardware store has many long-handled rakes.

7. The man bought plaid pants and a green shirt.

8. The new student was very shy but quite nice.

Wake Up, Brain!!

Name: _______________________________

Geography

1. What continents border the Mediterranean Sea?

   ____

   ____

2. What direction is Russia from the equator?

   ____

Math

List all the factors for each number.

3. 22 _______________________________

4. 63 _______________________________

5. 72 _______________________________

DID YOU KNOW?

A visitor to Central or South America can hear the call of the male howler monkey from more than three miles away.

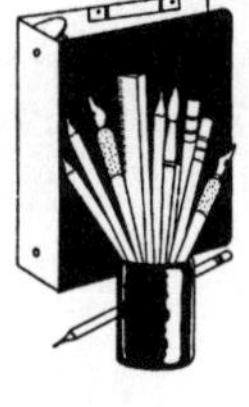

      ECS Learning Systems, Inc.

Wake Up, Brain!!

Name: ____

Grammar

1. chemical reactions take place when won or more substances is changes to knew substances

   ____

   ____

2. chemical reactions include's the reactants. The substances about too react. And the products?

   ____

   ____

Spelling

Write the words that are spelled correctly.

3. apearance   appearance   apperance   _______________________

4. chesst   cheest   chest   _______________________

5. ade   aid   ayde   _______________________

Language

Write the abbreviation for each of the following words:

6. boulevard ____

7. drive ____

8. apartment ____

          ECS Learning Systems, Inc.

Wake Up, Brain!!

Name: _______________________________

Geography

1. Which of the following is NOT an ocean?

☐ Arctic ☐ Bering ☐ Indian ☐ Pacific

2. What country is the closest southern neighbor for most of the United States?

____

Math

Write the prime factorization of each number.

3. 26 _______________________________

4. 35 _______________________________

5. 28 _______________________________

DID YOU KNOW?

It would take 220 Rhode Islands to fill up the state of Texas.

ECS Learning Systems, Inc.

Wake Up, Brain!!

Name: ___________________________________

Grammar

1. the law of conservation of mass states that matter is'nt not created or destroyed it is conserved

   ____

   ____

2. radioactivity is discovered bout one hundred years ago

   ____

   ____

Spelling

Write the words that are spelled correctly.

3. sammple   sampple   sample   _______________________

4. wrapped   wrapt   wraped   _______________________

5. introdused   introduced   intruduct   _______________________

Language

Write the abbreviation for each of the following words:

6. route   ____

7. doctor   ____

8. junior   ____

     ECS Learning Systems, Inc.

Wake Up, Brain!!

Name: ____

Geography

1. What direction from the Mississippi River are the Rocky Mountains?

   ____

2. What oceans border the United States?

   ____

Math

Compute.

3. 1000 g = _______________ kg

4. 3000 g = _______________ kg

5. 3500 g = _______________ kg

DID YOU KNOW?

Charles Sherwood Stratton was 3'4" tall and performed in
P.T. Barnum's circus under the stage name of "Tom Thumb."

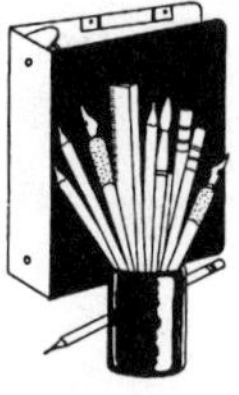

     ECS Learning Systems, Inc.   *Wake Up, Brain!!* • Grade 6

# Wake Up, Brain!!

Name: ____

Grammar

1. radioactivity has leaded too majer advances inn nuclear weapons. And nuclear energy

   ____

   ____

2. their is small amounts of radioactive materials all around us, you cant sea here taste touch
   or even smell them?

   ____

   ____

Spelling

Write the words that are spelled correctly.

3. menstion   mention   menshun   _______________________

4. pasenger   pasennger   passenger   _______________________

5. shert   shirt   shirrt   _______________________

Language

Write contractions for the following words:

6. was not   _______________________

7. he had   _______________________

8. I will   _______________________

        ECS Learning Systems, Inc.

Wake Up, Brain!!

Name: ____

Geography

1. Which state is south of North Dakota?

   ____

2. The Bering Sea touches the U.S. on the borders of what state?

   ____

Math

Compute.

3. _________________ L = 1600 ml

4. _________________ L = 1000 ml

5. _________________ L = 500 ml

DID YOU KNOW?

If you order a wahoo sandwich for lunch, the filling will be made of a tropical fish similar to tuna.

     ECS Learning Systems, Inc.   *Wake Up, Brain!!* • Grade 6   103

Wake Up, Brain!!

Name: ____

Grammar

1. you gots to hold your breath when passing a graveyard or the gosts will haunt you mary told me

   ____

   ____

2. many people who can not here has learned to communicate quiet well

   ____

   ____

Spelling

Write the words that are spelled correctly.

3. choise	choice	choisse	_______________
4. crawled	crauled	cralled	_______________
5. metter	metor	meter	_______________

Language

Use **good** or **well** properly in the following sentences.

6. People know Kelly is a _________________________ artist.

7. She has drawn some very _________________________ pictures.

8. She draws people very _________________________.

   ECS Learning Systems, Inc.

Wake Up, Brain!!

Name: ____

Geography

1. What state has the longer Pacific Ocean border?

    ☐ Washington   ☐ Oregon

2. Which state is bordered by two oceans?

    ____

Math

Write as a mixed fraction.

3. $4\frac{1}{4}$ = _______________________

4. $9\frac{2}{5}$ = _______________________

5. $8\frac{1}{3}$ = _______________________

6. $3\frac{7}{8}$ = _______________________

DID YOU KNOW?

America's oldest standing church steeple was built in 1729 and can be seen at the Old South Church in Boston.

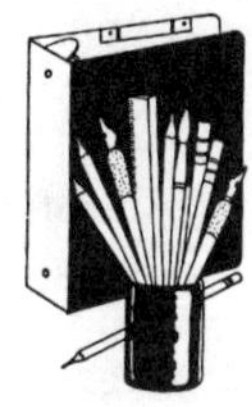

          ECS Learning Systems, Inc.

Answer Key

Page 6
1. Answers will vary.
2. Answers will vary.
3. watch
4. within
5. themselves
6. begin
7. Answers will vary but must include four pairs of appropriate synonyms.

Page 7
1. Hawaii, Honolulu; Alaska, Juneau
2. Europe, Asia, North America
3. 0.9; 349.04; 19.17; 5.89
4. 15; 3; 622.2

Page 8
1. Answers will vary.
2. Answers will vary.
3. society
4. eager
5. fort
6. <u>studies</u>, class/week/space
7. <u>mowed</u>, Doug/grass
8. <u>won</u>, Chelsea/game/HORSE

Page 9
1. F
2. T
3. F
4. 4,600
5. 28.04
6. 0.3

Page 10
1. Answers will vary.
2. Answers will vary.
3. lips
4. motor
5. shut
6. rain, day
7. rain, night
8. rain, coats

Page 11
1. North Dakota
2. east, St. Paul
3. $13.50
4. Yes

Page 12
1. Answers will vary.
2. Answers will vary.
3. asleep
4. blend
5. magic
6. Jul., Aug., Sept., Oct., Nov., Dec.

Page 13
1. Florida
2. California
3. $2.37 (rounded to nearest cent)
4. $16.80
5. $8.00

Page 14
1. Answers will vary.
2. Answers will vary.
3. native
4. nodded
5. tent
6. wolf, mouse, wax, tooth, echo, party

Page 15
1. New Mexico
2. Louisiana
3. 41,654 inches
4. 15.624
5. 1,887 mm
6. 0.5088

Page 16
1. 727 Northgate Mile, Seattle, Washington 83505
2. June 23, 2003
3. boiling
4. fractional
5. habits
6. sent
7. goes
8. performed

Page 17
1. Illinois River
2. Tallahassee
3. 2.0042
4. .0073

Page 18
1. Answers will vary.
2. port
3. reflected
4. extra
5. It
6. We
7. Jay

Page 19
1. U.S.
2. Atlantic, Arctic
3. 1, 3, 9
4. 1, 2, 3, 4, 6, 12
5. 1, 7

Page 20
1. Answers will vary.
2. Answers will vary.
3. harbor
4. tank
5. coffee
6-8. Answers will vary but should contain an appropriate simile.

Page 21
1. Phoenix
2. New York
3. 3 hundred thousand
4. 30 thousand
5. 3 million

Page 22
1. Answers will vary.
2. Answers will vary.
3. social
4. swift
5. adventure
6. Jeff and Susan mowed the very long grass.

Page 23
1. Texas
2. Nevada
3. 1, 2
4. 1, 2, 5, 10

   ECS Learning Systems, Inc.

Answer Key

Page 24
1. Answers will vary.
2. Answers will vary.
3. personal
4. prize
5. sunlight
6. Julie raked all the leaves while Connie put them in a bag.

Page 25
1. North, South, East, West
2. T
3. 1, 2, 4
4. 1
5. 1, 5

Page 26
1. Answers will vary.
2. Answers will vary.
3. bare
4. lock
5. relations
6. We went to the baseball game and watched them lose.
7. We went to the fair and rode all the rides.

Page 27
1. Madagascar
2. Amazon River
3. e = 4
4. m = 10
5. q = 33

Page 28
1. Answers will vary.
2. Answers will vary.
3. bouquet
4. chain
5. features
6. We could go to the show or go bowling.

Page 29
1. Northeast
2. Rio Grande
3. 45
4. 48
5. 4

Page 30
1. Answers will vary.
2. Answers will vary.
3. castle
4. hadn't
5. knocked
6. class-C, Europe-P, France-P, country-C, teacher-C, school-C

Page 31
1. Belize, Costa Rica, El Salvador, Guatemala, Honduras, Nicaragua, Panama
2. 171.2
3. 4,576
4. 7.83
5. c
6. b

Page 32
1. Answers will vary.
2. Answers will vary.
3. merely
4. physical
5. stroke
6. girl-C, Brazil-P, Rosa-P, Snake River-P, continent-C, principal-C

Page 33
1. North and South Pole
2. The Gulf of Carpentaria
3. 442 r13
4. 1080 r2
5. 299 r20
6. 984 r7

Page 34
1. Answers will vary.
2. Answers will vary.
3. ability
4. device
5. owner
6. deer, watches, monkeys, sheep, wolves, berries

Page 35
1. Montana
2. Russia
3. 14
4. 2

Page 36
1. Answers will vary.
2. Answers will vary.
3. taught
4. delightful
5. refrigerator
6. women, calves, babies, oxen, feet, tomatoes

Page 37
1. Amazon
2. Rome
3. 256
4. 34
5. 2001
6. 802

Page 38
1. Answers will vary.
2. Answers will vary.
3. weak
4. federal
5. ordinary
6. men's coats, girl's hat, fox's ear, women's flowers, baby's (babies') clothes, deer's feet

Page 39
1. east and west
2. Asia
3. 3 and 19
4. 3 and 7

Page 40
1. Answers will vary.
2. Answers will vary.
3. sorry
4. cage
5. monkey
6. bees' honey, family's car, woman's house, roses' thorns, flower's petals, dog's fleas

Page 41
1. north and south
2. South America
3. 1968
4. 1963, 30%

Answer Key

Page 42
1. Answers will vary.
2. Answers will vary.
3. account
4. board
5. communicate
6. lighthouse
7. dolphin
8. ship

Page 43
1. Africa
2. Austin
3. 45.05
4. 44.66
5. 33.132

Page 44
1. Answers will vary.
2. Answers will vary.
3. mirror
4. outline
5. deck
6. stores
7. necklaces
8. birdhouses

Page 45
1. Asia
2. Yes
3. <
4. >
5. >
6. <

Page 46
1. Answers will vary.
2. Answers will vary.
3. police
4. species
5. stranger
6. Underlined
7. Not underlined
8. Not underlined

Page 47
1. Asia
2. No
3. 0.8
4. 0.8
5. 0.9
6. 5.00

Page 48
1. Answers will vary.
2. Answers will vary.
3. electrons
4. foreign
5. fought
6. cheerfully
7. bright, early
8. gracefully

Page 49
1. Canada
2. Strait of Gibraltar
3. 54.7
4. 7.68
5. 140

Page 50
1. Answers will vary.
2. Answers will vary.
3. industrial
4. accident
5. department
6. blew
7. froze
8. wrote
9. sang
10. spoke

Page 51
1. U.S. and Mexico
2. Asia and North America
3. 3.02
4. 8.963

Page 52
1. Answers will vary.
2. flash
3. whenever
4. grade
5. study
6. fix
7. fish
8. cry
9. watch
10. wash

Page 53
1. Russia
2. New York
3. 0.407 or about 41%
4. 12:52 p.m.

Page 54
1. Answers will vary.
2. Answers will vary.
3. perform
4. library
5. wolves
6. He/She/It; We/They; We/They; He/She/It

Page 55
1. north and south
2. The Andes Mountains
3. 1963
4. 35%

Page 56
1. Answers will vary.
2. Answers will vary.
3. maybe
4. future
5. fifteen
6. Example: beautifully
7. Example: fitfully
8. Example: quickly

Page 57
1. Canada
2. New York
3. 12n
4. 12n
5. $6n

Page 58
1. Answers will vary.
2. Answers will vary.
3. thermos
4. dictionary
5. maintenance
6. were/are; are/were; am; saw/sees

Page 59
1. True
2. the Bering Strait
3. 3.4666 grams

Page 60
1. Answers will vary.
2. Answers will vary.
3. formula
4. measure
5. potato
6. mow, mean, copy, drink, work, seal, see, go

 ECS Learning Systems, Inc.

Answer Key

Page 61
1. True
2. Maryland and Delaware
3. 109.3413
4. 7.7131
5. 267.2944
6. 21.154

Page 62
1. Answers will vary.
2. Answers will vary.
3. obey
4. ocean
5. poem
6. African
7. Polish
8. English
9. American

Page 63
1. Asia
2. South America
3. North America
4. 420 gal/day, 153,300 gal/year

Page 64
1. Answers will vary.
2. Answers will vary.
3. owner
4. program
5. awoke
6. go
7. teach
8. see

Page 65
1. Taiwan
2. The Appalachian Mountains
3. 5, 10, 15, 20, 25
4. 8, 16, 24, 32, 40
5. 17, 34, 51, 68, 85
6. 20, 40, 60, 80, 100

Page 66
1. Answers will vary.
2. Answers will vary.
3. license
4. prompt
5. engineer
6. children's books
7. jar's lid
8. deer's antlers

Page 67
1. the Strait of Gibraltar
2. Spain
3. 1968
4. 1963 and 1968

Page 68
1. Answers will vary.
2. Answers will vary.
3. bandana/bandanna
4. vacuum
5. pansy
6. team's coaches
7. stores' signs
8. spoon's handle

Page 69
1. Nile River
2. Mediterranean
3. 7
4. 7
5. 30

Page 70
1. Answers will vary.
2. Answers will vary.
3. course
4. develop
5. radical
6. women
7. calves
8. babies
9. tomatoes

Page 71
1. Asia, Antarctica, Australia, North America, South America
2. False
3. No
4. No, $27 more is needed.

Page 72
1. Answers will vary.
2. Answers will vary.
3. guess
4. shelves
5. sacrifice
6. fell, settled
7. stomped, yelled, jumped

Page 73
1. False
2. False
3. No, he must ride 33.3 km per day.
4. Yes

Page 74
1. Answers will vary.
2. Answers will vary.
3. create
4. desperate
5. memories
6. homework
7. title
8. car

Page 75
1. False
2. False
3. three million
4. fifty thousand
5. seventy million

Page 76
1. Answers will vary.
2. Answers will vary.
3. cities
4. centuries
5. dairies
6. seam
7. tacks
8. ours

Page 77
1. False
2. True
3. No
4. Yes
5. Yes
6. No

Page 78
1. Answers will vary.
2. Answers will vary.
3. married
4. countries
5. surround
6. drew–T
7. laughed–I
8. was frustrated–I
9. ate–T

ECS Learning Systems, Inc.

Answer Key

Page 79
1. Antarctica
2. True
3. 365 x .24 = 87.6;
   365 – 87.6 = 277.4 days longer

Page 80
1. Answers will vary.
2. Answers will vary.
3. lying
4. mixture
5. stitch
6. has
7. has
8. have

Page 81
1. N. America, S. America, Europe,
   Asia, Africa, Antarctica, Australia
2. 3 x 7 = 21 days
3. 6 x 7 = 42 days
4. 15 x 7 = 105 days

Page 82
1. Answers will vary.
2. Answers will vary.
3. disloyal
4. pronounce
5. heard
6. <u>un</u>happy
7. <u>mis</u>lead
8. <u>re</u>search

Page 83
1. San Francisco, CA
2. False
3. 2
4. 5
5. 11

Page 84
1. Answers will vary.
2. Answers will vary.
3. invited
4. pioneers
5. predicate
6. carried
7. studied
8. destroyed

Page 85
1. Western
2. North America, Asia, Africa
3. 32 x $.05 = $1.60 ÷ $.10 = 16 dimes
4. 40 x $.05 = $2.00 ÷ $.10 = 20 dimes
5. 100 x $.05 = $5.00 ÷ $.10 = 50 dimes

Page 86
1. Answers will vary.
2. Answers will vary.
3. remind
4. reptiles
5. captured
6. have
7. had
8. have

Page 87
1. Pacific, Atlantic, Arctic, Indian
2. Atlantic, Arctic
3. No, he'll be $3.50 short.

Page 88
1. Answers will vary.
2. Answers will vary.
3. communication
4. loose
5. differ
6. described
7. fell
8. made

Page 89
1. Antarctica
2. Asia, Europe
3. $1.25
4. 249

Page 90
1. Answers will vary.
2. Answers will vary.
3. diving
4. grinned
5. package
6. said
7. flew
8. brought

Page 91
1. Pacific
2. California
3. Pacific
4. 101.5
5. 209.33
6. 3.50

Page 92
1. Answers will vary.
2. Answers will vary.
3. medicine
4. construction
5. gradually
6. some, toy, sharp
7. new
8. long, brown

Page 93
1. Frankfort
2. Sacramento
3. Dover
4. 7 hours 43 minutes
5. 8:15 p.m.

Page 94
1. Answers will vary.
2. Answers will vary.
3. specific
4. trunk
5. author
6. most, major, several, good
7. red, ugly
8. TV, many, excellent, trained

Page 95
1. Providence
2. Salem
3. Atlanta
4. 10:45 a.m.
5. Monday, 3:47 a.m.

Page 96
1. Answers will vary.
2. Answers will vary.
3. outer
4. pump
5. song
6. hardware, many, long-handled
7. plaid, green
8. new, shy, nice

   ECS Learning Systems, Inc.

Answer Key

Page 97
1. Africa, Europe, Asia
2. North
3. 1, 2, 11, 22
4. 1, 3, 7, 9, 21, 63
5. 1, 2, 3, 4, 6, 8, 9, 12, 18, 24, 36, 72

Page 98
1. Answers will vary.
2. Answers will vary.
3. appearance
4. chest
5. aid
6. Blvd./blvd.
7. Dr.
8. apt.

Page 99
1. Bering Sea
2. Mexico
3. 2 x 13
4. 5 x 7
5. 2 x 2 x 7

Page 100
1. Answers will vary.
2. Answers will vary.
3. sample
4. wrapped
5. introduced
6. rte.
7. Dr.
8. Jr.

Page 101
1. west
2. Pacific, Atlantic, Arctic
3. 1 kg
4. 3 kg
5. 3.5 kg

Page 102
1. Answers will vary.
2. Answers will vary.
3. mention
4. passenger
5. shirt
6. wasn't
7. he'd
8. I'll

Page 103
1. South Dakota
2. Alaska
3. 1.6 L
4. 1 L
5. 0.5 L

Page 104
1. Answers will vary.
2. Answers will vary.
3. choice
4. crawled
5. meter
6. good
7. good
8. well

Page 105
1. Washington
2. Alaska
3. 17/4
4. 47/5
5. 25/3
6. 31/8

Notes

ECS Learning Systems, Inc.

About the Authors

After graduating from the University of Utah, **Michelle Ball** (right) lived in Salt Lake City before returning to her hometown of Idaho Falls, Idaho. She has three children, Conrad, Rebecca, and Patrick. Her husband, Doug, is a great support in her life and has always valued her love for teaching. He is an active part of her school life and known in the neighborhood as "Mrs. Ball's Husband."

Michelle's 15 years of teaching experiences in kindergarten, second, and third grades provided a sound foundation for her current position as a teacher in a multi-age classroom. "Teaching three grades at once has definitely enhanced my life (my dear friend and co-author's daughter was my student). Working in a multi-age classroom has provided opportunities to develop organizational skills and teaching strategies that benefit my students. Working with children has given me countless joys. My students have enriched my life beyond measure."

Barbara Morris (left) grew up and received her education in Idaho. A career in banking took her to Utah and California before she and her husband, Tony, became parents and moved back "home" to Idaho to raise their only child, Jennifer. As a new parent, "Barb" developed her own publishing skills and eventually built a small, in-home desktop publishing business.

Barb met Michelle as she enrolled Jennifer in Michelle's multi-grade classroom. Eventually, their relationship developed into a bond of friendship that enhanced both lives and fulfilled their individual goals and dreams. As a full-time office manager for a local hospital, Barb had little time to volunteer in the classroom, but had a desire to stay involved with her child's education. She offered her desktop publishing skills to Michelle, who sketched out student worksheets, literature studies, and classroom management tools. Barb converted them into the original student-friendly and teacher-helpful *Wake Up, Brain!!*, which developed into the new series for grades 1 through 6.

ECS Learning Systems, Inc.